How to Achieve Better Student Retention in Adult Education

Secrets for Becoming an Exceptional Adult Ed Instructor Who Inspires Learners to Persist and Succeed!

Second Edition

COACH TEDDY EDOUARD

Copyright © 2025 Teddy Edouard
All rights reserved.
ISBN: 978-1-63901-849-9

This book is designed to offer guidance on teacher development and adult learning. But its teaching should not be taken as legal advice and services. If you need legal help, consult a licensed legal professional.

While Coaching for Better Learning (CBL) LLC has made every effort to provide accurate information at the time of publication, neither the publisher nor the author assumes any responsibility for errors and changes that happen after the release of this book. The author and the publisher have no control over and do not assume any responsibility and liability for third-party websites and their content.

Copyright ©2025 Coaching For Better Learning, LLC

Copyright ©2025 Teddy Edouard

Second Edition

All rights reserved. No portion of this book may be reproduced without written permission of CBL and the author.

DEDICATION

To all the passionate adult education instructors out there, especially those who want to be remarkable. And to everyone, including support staff, who is committed to improving the lives of adult learners. I wrote this book for you.

ACKNOWLEDGMENTS

Thank you to my family and all my friends!
You motivate me to get better day by day.

Table of Contents

Dedication 4

Acknowledgments 5

Introduction 8

Chapter 1: Understanding Our Calling 13

Chapter 2: Foundation: Key Theories That Influence Adult Learning 21

Chapter 3: Taking Matters Into Your Own Hands 33

Chapter 4: Identifying The Warning Signs 40

Chapter 5: Building A System For Student Engagement And Retention 46

Chapter 6: Raising Your Learning- Facilitation Game ... 54

Chapter 7: Flexible Knowledge And Transferable Skills ... 65

Chapter 8: Test Preparation (Game Day!) 77

Chapter 9: Real-World Learning- Facilitation Guidelines ... 84

Conclusion 96

Index 98

References 99

More Textbooks By CBL 103

About The Author 103

INTRODUCTION

Become the kind of leader that people would follow voluntarily, even if you had no title or position.

– Brian Tracy

Imagine this scenario: You start your semester all excited. Your technical training or adult ed class—whether that's HiSET, GED, ASE, ABE, ESL/ELL, CTE, or ITE—is at full capacity. You work hard to choose materials, plan lessons, and s for your learners, hoping to keep them happy.

After a few weeks, you realize half your learners have missed at least one class and several have completely stopped attending. You know the writing is on the wall. Things aren't looking too good, are they?

I have faced this issue multiple times. My mistake was assuming my class was so important that if learners knew what they wanted, they would make sure to attend. While I put in extra effort to meet key standards and ensured learners were aware of the attendance policy, that still was not enough to move the needle in the right direction.

Losing learners made me question my skills as an adult ed instructor. I bet it makes you feel the same way too. But how can you prevent losing learners or avoid this issue altogether? Unfortunately, there isn't a magic answer to that question.

However, the solution may lie in how we perceive our role and the kind of system we establish to motivate our learners to come for more. It also depends on our ability to help learners change the story they tell themselves, transforming their perceptions of themselves, learning, testing, and success. Is that possible? Yes, and I'll elaborate on that a little later.

Realistically, you may not always keep a 100 percent retention rate. But your retention and attendance rate should not be under 50 percent either, with learners dropping out from your courses like sand through a sieve!

The bad news is that some learners will struggle to stay engaged due to various factors beyond our control. The good news is that there are many ways to support learners—by leading, motivating, and inspiring them to keep going.

But to do so, we have to raise the bar and focus on what matters the most: *helping our learners develop connections and salable skills.*

But first, here are some things to keep in mind before we delve deeper into the subject:

As adult educators, we have an obligation to guide and inspire our learners to stick around so they can gain the skills and knowledge to navigate life's challenges.

- Adult ed teachers are dedicated and work hard, but our efforts will have minimal to no impact if we are unable to encourage learners to return for more. In other words, we won't see the fruits of our labor unless learners stay engaged until their learning changes them for the better.

- Losing a significant number of learners within a few weeks might demotivate the rest of the class and cause learners to skip classes—until they eventually stop attending.

- Learners are in search of "better": better skills, better connections, and better community. They also have problems they want solved, so they need to learn skills to improve their lives outside the classroom.

- We are leaders and influencers. Thus, we have to lead, influence, empower, and inspire our learners.

- We need learners as much as they need us. A good retention rate is a win-win situation. It keeps our programs in business.

- Adult ed program leaders respect and value educators who can keep their learners engaged and eager to stay in class to achieve learning outcomes. These educators are assets no program director wants to lose.

What does all this mean? It means maintaining above-average student retention is beneficial to you, your learners, and your program. Everyone wins. But how can you make this happen? That's exactly what this retention book is all about.

> Wherever we are, whatever we're doing and wherever we are going, we owe it to ourselves, to our art, to the world to do it well.
>
> **– Ryan Holiday**

What's New in This Edition

This updated edition introduces valuable content for adult educators, including more insights on hybrid and online teaching, advanced test-taking strategies, and expanded discussions on key learning theories. Notably, the edition includes a summary and limitations of **andragogy,** a look into the **theory of margin**, and a deeper exploration of **transformative learning**. These theories offer educators more tools to improve student engagement and retention in both traditional and online classrooms.

Here is a brief overview of what each chapter covers:

- **Chapter 1: Understanding Our Calling**

  Unveils the powerful mission behind adult education and the transformative impact of a strong teaching philosophy.

- **Chapter 2: Foundation: Key Theories That Influence Adult Learning**

    Summarizes important learning theories (including **andragogy**) and their impact on retention and persistence.

- **Chapter 3: Taking Matters into Your Own Hands**

    Encourages educators to create their own retention strategies, even in the absence of a formal program system.

- **Chapter 4: Identifying the Warning Signs**

    Identifies signs of student disengagement and how to respond to them.

- **Chapter 5: Building a System for Student Engagement and Retention**

    Guides educators on how to create effective systems that enhance student retention and success.

- **Chapter 6: Raising Your Learning-Facilitation Game**

    Offers techniques to improve the learning experience and keep students engaged.

- **Chapter 7: Flexible Knowledge and Transferable Skills**

    Focuses on teaching skills for real-world application.

- **Chapter 8: Test Preparation (Game Day!)**

    Expands on strategies to help students manage test-taking anxiety and improve performance.

- **Chapter 9: Real-World Oriented Learning-Facilitation Guidelines**

  Provides a roadmap for creating real-world learning experiences that build 21st-century skills.

- **Conclusion:**

  Reinforces the impact of effective teaching.

- **Disclaimer:**

  This book does not offer quick fixes. Instead, it presents a philosophy and process to help you teach with greater impact. The system works if you can stick to it and are willing to take the risk of becoming an exceptional adult ed professional.

Still interested? Great! Then let's start at the beginning:

- Why did you pursue a career in adult education?

- Why do you choose to do what you do?

- What's your motivation for doing what you do?

CHAPTER 1

Understanding Our Calling

> No individual has any right to come into the world and go out of it without leaving behind him distinct and legitimate reasons for having passed through it.
>
> **– George Washington Carver**

Before we dive into the topic of learner retention, let's first understand our role as adult educators.

Adult educators work diligently every day to make our society a better place by guiding learners toward a path to success and a better tomorrow. Their efforts are crucial in combating issues like illiteracy, high unemployment rates, and crimes within our communities. In fact, Harlow (2003) reveals in a Bureau of Justice Statistics Special Report that three-quarters of state-incarcerated individuals either did not complete high school or have low literacy. Given these statistics, state and local officials should consider supporting adult education.

> This profession is more than a job—it's a calling.

Adult educators play a vital role in guiding learners closer to achieving their dreams, but there is a problem. According to Maslow's hierarchy of needs, adult ed classes are not considered a basic need. This implies that our adult programs and classes are NOT indispensable. However, we can make our services crucial by offering adult learners what they truly need—and a compelling reason to persist.

Why Support Adult Education?

Higher Tax Revenue

For every 400,000 adults who earn a high school diploma, there is a gain of **$2.5 billion** in tax revenue.

McLendon, L., Jones, D. and M. Rosin. (2011). The Return on Investment from Adult Education and Training. McGraw Hill Research Foundation.

Poverty Connection

Low literacy contributes to **poverty cycles**, **poor health**, and **low educational attainment**, worsening economic inequality.

Nietzel, M. T. (2020). Low literacy levels among U.S. adults. Forbes.

Increased Earnings

Median lifetime **earnings grow** with higher levels of education.

Georgetown University Center on Education and the Workforce. (2011). The college payoff: Education, occupations, lifetime earnings.

Increased Independence

Spending on **welfare programs** is **lower** for individuals with higher levels of education.

College Board. (2023). Education Pays 2023. Research.collegeboard.org.

Figure 1: The Economic and Social Benefits of Adult Education

Understanding What Learners Truly Value

Let's admit it: adult learners don't necessarily value adult ed classes in the same way we do, and their interests can vary significantly from ours. While we may be passionate about our topic, what these learners often need are practical and life-changing skills in reading, writing, speaking, and mathematical thinking that directly impact their everyday lives. For example, our lessons might seem appealing to us, but the materials might be irrelevant and mundane to learners. So, what can we do about this disconnect?

The answer is to focus on **transformative learning**—empowering learners to rewrite their life stories. This approach, which we'll explore further in Chapter 2, goes beyond test preparation and focuses on real-world success. When we align our teaching with what learners truly need, we provide them with a ticket to success.

This type of calling is not about a learner-teacher relationship of tests/exams and compliance. Instead, it requires a learner-mentor relationship based on trust, choice, and care, which fosters long-term growth. In other words, it's about changing students for the better and helping them develop skills they can use in the marketplace with confidence.

> Our goal should not just be about giving learners what they need to pass an exam but about teaching them transferable skills that will serve them throughout their lives.

It's like the familiar adage: "Give a man a fish, and he eats for a day; teach a man to fish, and he eats for a lifetime." Not only do we want to provide learners with the knowledge required to pass a test but also with skills and resources that they can use for the rest of their lives.

As adult educators, we have the potential to create more meaningful change than we often realize. Our responsibility is to give learners what they need to succeed independently in the real world.

We have a calling to transform our adult students into lifelong learners and support them in becoming the professionals they've dreamed of becoming—or at least getting them closer to their goals, one class and one lesson at a time. Learners must work hard and take ownership of their learning journey.

The Promise We Should Make To Learners

Making the promise to learners that a degree or diploma is all they need is not enough in today's world. In reality, succeeding in the current job market requires 21st-century skills that go beyond what standardized tests can measure. According to the World Economic Forum (2015), thriving in today's economy demands a different mix of skills than in the past, including critical thinking, problem-solving, and collaboration.

> The leader is one who, out of the clutter, brings simplicity... out of discord, harmony... and out of difficulty, opportunity.
>
> **– Albert Einstein**

Therefore, what learners truly need is knowledge and practical skills that will help them secure better jobs, create businesses, and ultimately improve their lives. They seek financial stability, safety, respect, and a sense of belonging—goals that can't be achieved through certification alone.

Addressing the learning needs of adult students is critical to their success in the real world. But you won't be able to meet the needs of learners who stop attending your program. The key to making a meaningful impact on your learners starts with your ability to offer them a learning experience that keeps them coming back for more, one class after another.

Our lessons should tap into their passions, desires, and talents, aligning with their personal and professional goals. That's why finding a connection between the lessons we teach and what students need is incredibly important. Sustaining their interest and success is critical.

This is where the challenge—or the beauty—comes in. Different learners have unique needs, leading them to seek out various places. Some may not even know what they want, so it's our job to help them figure it out before they move on.

Regardless of the destination each learner wants to reach, our promise to our learners should be to take them on an inspiring educational journey that brings them closer to their dreams (not the dream we have for them!), one semester at a time.

Adult learners are not impressed with standard lessons designed for average students. They seek learning experiences that are fulfilling and provide value. They crave inspiration, leadership, and skills that will help them stand out in the competitive world.

Therefore, we must prepare learners for real-world challenges by fostering **deep-structure learning** and promoting **soft skills** essential in today's job market, including communication, problem-solving, and adaptability.

By consistently keeping our promise to lead and inspire, we can hope our learners will be compelled to do the same by being committed on their educational journey.

Making an Impact

To truly fulfill our promise to learners, we have two options in adult education: we can settle for being average, traditional, and anonymous, or we can take a chance at greatness, uniqueness, and excellence for the sake of the learners who put so much trust in us. Which one will you choose? We must go beyond traditional teaching methods. Making an impact means challenging the status quo and ensuring our learners gain skills that extend beyond the classroom.

> The linchpin resists the pressure to conform and comply. Instead, she works without a map, solves interesting problems, leads, connects and creates an impact.
>
> – Seth Godin

Every adult ed teacher has the opportunity to challenge the status quo. But this opportunity comes with a cost. There's a price for leading and teaching in a transformational way—for refusing to be average, fit in, and settle. It demands courage, persistence, and a commitment to excellence.

The best way to teach in a transformational way is not to let our expectations or biases about our learners get in the way. Instead, we should set the bar high for every learner. Promote a race to the top that involves teamwork, problem-solving, and critical thinking. Our work will speak for itself through the higher-order skills our learners demonstrate across all subject areas.

Raising the bar high also means pushing students to perform beyond what the test expects or requires of them. Teach for mastery. The more we teach for mastery and focus on deep-structure learning, the easier the test will be.

Learners who strive to achieve mastery will:

- Set ambitious goals, prioritize, and focus on meaningful pursuits.

- Read, understand, summarize, and present various texts, both verbal and in writing.

- Express themselves with tact and ask insightful questions.

- Read between the lines and make inferences.

- Show agency and the ability to learn new concepts and skills on their own.

- Apply math problems and scientific information in a variety of contexts or situations.

- Use evidence, data, and abstract reasoning to make generalizations.

- Think critically and solve complex problems with a growth mindset.

- Connect classroom learning and skills to real-world situations and current trends.

- Show emotional intelligence and self-control.

- Develop soft and irreplaceable skills and competencies.

- Develop and explore their talents.

Systems Win Championships

Helping learners achieve mastery requires a system. A strong **instructional system** ensures that learners are not just attending classes but are engaged, motivated, and consistently making progress. It builds a classroom culture where learners feel they belong and believe effective learning is within reach.

There is a major difference between telling learners they need to attend classes versus instilling a desire to learn in them. There's also a big difference between teaching them to pass a test and piquing their curiosity so they have a desire for knowledge and self-improvement. To drive our learners to that point, we must create a system that inspires them as opposed to using rules or requirements to manage them.

That's why instructors should create effective instructional systems. As adult ed educators, we can build a system much bigger than ourselves—a system that keeps learners engaged and equips them with the skills they need to succeed today. Just as great coaches cultivate winning teams, we must create learning environments where students recognize the value of what we are building and are eager to follow our lead.

This book will show you how to create a system that works for you and your learners. This can only be achieved through structure, strategy, and a strong commitment to continuous improvement. In other words, we must focus on teaching for real change and lasting impact.

> Paint a picture of the future.
> Go there. People will follow.
>
> – Seth Godin

CHAPTER 2

Foundation: Key Theories That Influence Adult Learning

Change is the end result of all true learning.

– Leo Buscaglia

In this chapter, I'll summarize and discuss three learning theories that should influence your planning and teaching: **andragogy**, the **theory of margin**, and **transformative learning**. Understanding these insights will help you identify issues and make educated decisions to address them to promote learner persistence.

The Theory of Andragogy

What Is Andragogy?

Andragogy describes the characteristics of adult learners and offers insights into promoting effective adult learning. The term was introduced by Malcolm Knowles, who identified six key assumptions about how adults learn. These assumptions provide the foundation for the theory. Let's go over them one by one.

1. The Need to Know or Purpose of Learning

Adults require a clear understanding of *why* they should learn something. When they see the topic's relevance to their personal or professional lives, their motivation to learn increases. Therefore, forcing someone to learn usually makes the experience less effective.

2. A Preference for Self-Direction

Most adults take responsibility for their own lives, including their learning. They learn better when they control the learning process and learn something that aligns with their interests, goals, or personal needs.

3. Learning from Prior Experience

Prior knowledge and life experiences can serve as a foundation for new learning in adult education. Adults have a wealth of prior experiences that may facilitate new learning.

4. Readiness to Learn

Adults are ready to learn because they want new knowledge or skills to handle real-life challenges. Their readiness is often linked to their goals, such as advancing in a career, managing household responsibilities, or adapting to life changes. When learning is relevant to their immediate needs, they become more engaged and motivated.

5. Orientation to Learning

While younger learners often focus on acquiring abstract and general knowledge, adults prefer learning that helps solve problems they face in their personal or professional lives. They are more motivated when the content is directly related to their everyday challenges.

6. Internal Motivation

Unlike younger learners who often learn due to external pressures, such as school and parents' requirements, adult learners are primarily driven by internal factors. They pursue knowledge because of personal goals, interests, and a desire for self-improvement.

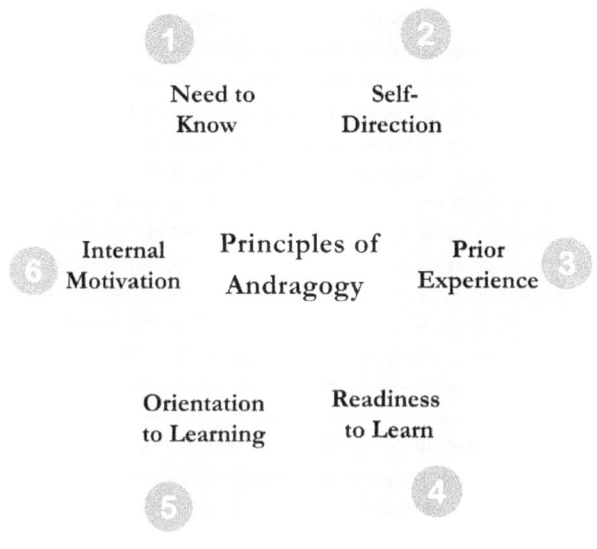

Figure 2: Diagram of Principles of Andragogy

Limitations of Andragogy

While Knowles' theory of andragogy has been instrumental in shaping adult education, it does have some limitations.

1. Lack of Empirical Evidence

According to Rachal (2002), not all of the assumptions in andragogy are backed by research. While the principles make sense in theory, more studies are needed to verify their application in different contexts and learning environments.

2. Variability in Learner Characteristics

Clardy (2005) argues that "adults participate in educational programs with different motives and preferences for learning, not with an invariant andragogical outlook." In other words, not all adults prefer self-directed learning. Some may prefer instructor-led approaches because they lack the confidence to direct their own learning. Some may also struggle with motivation, particularly those facing challenging life circumstances, such as trauma, which may hinder their learning.

3. Gaps in Understanding How Learning Occurs

While andragogy highlights certain characteristics of adult learners, it doesn't fully explain how adults process, retain, and apply knowledge. Without this, it's difficult to promote information processing and learning or predict how adults might react to different teaching methods or environments.

Implication: Applying Andragogy in Practice

Now that we've explored Knowles' core assumptions and the theory's limitations, let's review practical ways to apply andragogy in the adult education classroom. Knowles outlines the **andragogical process design**, which consists of steps aimed at improving the adult learning experience.

Step #1: Preparation

The first step of the process is to prepare learners for the program or course they will be joining. Your students must know what they will be learning, why it's important, and what the expectations are. For example, in a CTE training program, explaining how new software skills will directly impact job performance and career advancement helps adults understand the value of learning.

Step #2: Atmosphere

Learners tend to perform better in environments where they feel respected and valued. Foster an inclusive, nonjudgmental setting that encourages active participation. For example, arranging the classroom to encourage discussion and collaboration—like using small group activities or peer sharing—can make adults feel more comfortable engaging in learning.

Step #3: Planning

Generally, adults prefer to work with a clear purpose and plan. Planning the learning process should be a collaborative activity and a discussion about goals, outcomes, and methods. For instance, when organizing a course on financial literacy, you might ask learners to share their personal financial goals and incorporate them into the course content. This approach makes the learning experience feel more personalized and relevant.

Step #4: The "What" and the "Why"

Clarify what students will learn and why they need that knowledge. This is a key part of adult education—adults tend to be more motivated when they see a clear connection between what they are learning and their real-life challenges.

For example, if you're teaching a class on time management, the "what" could include specific skills like setting priorities, managing deadlines, or reducing stress. These are skills that adults can directly apply in their personal and professional lives.

Step #5: Objectives

Establish clear and measurable objectives to give learners a sense of purpose and help them stay motivated. For example, in a GED, HiSET, or ESL/ELL course focusing on reading, an objective could be comparing texts and answering questions correctly. This can be broken down into specific goals, such as understanding types of texts and identifying main ideas and supporting details. Each step builds the skills needed to succeed on the final test.

The Theory of Margin

The **theory of margin**, also known as the **power-load-margin**, is a concept developed by Howard McClusky in adult education. The theory suggests that adults require a balance between the "**load**" (the demands, challenges and pressures of life) they carry and the "**power**" (the time, energy, ability, resources and support available to meet those demands) they have to function effectively.

High margin: Power outweighs load, meaning learners have energy and capacity left to engage in learning and training.

Low margin: Load exceeds power, meaning learners are crushed under the weight of life challenges, making it difficult for them to engage in learning, even when they desperately need new skills and knowledge to do better.

> **The margin** is the space between load and power, and it determines an adult's capacity to participate in learning for personal and professional growth.

Margin = Load/Power

According to McClusky, the margin is determined by the **ratio between power and load**. To support adult learners, educators and institutions should aim to help learners increase their power (e.g., through flexible learning schedules and emotional support) and reduce load (e.g., by minimizing unnecessary stress or obstacles) to offer an optimal learning environment.

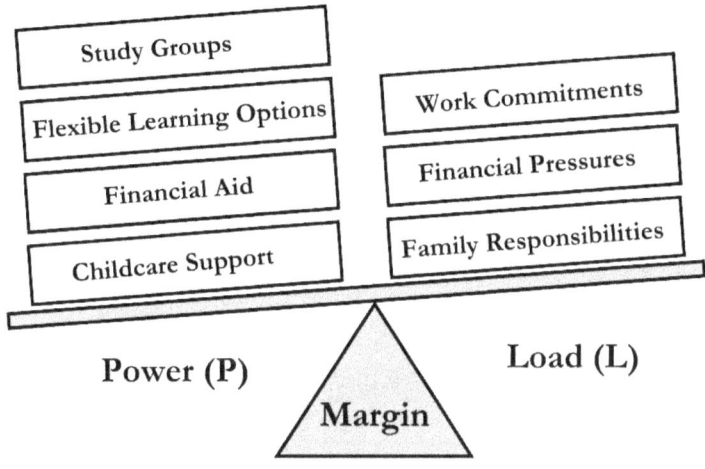

Figure 3: McClusky's Theory of Margin

Limitations of the Theory of Margin

While the theory of margin offers significant insights into how various life factors influence a learner's capacity to engage in learning, it does have certain limitations.

1. Lack of Specific Learning Framework

The theory addresses how social, physical, mental, and economic factors affect students' ability to learn and retain information. However, it does not explain how adults process, retain, and apply knowledge in specific learning environments.

2. Absence of Prescribed Teaching Strategies

While educators understand the importance of balancing load and power, the theory does not provide guidance on how to design effective instructional activities to support our learners' needs and objectives.

3. Limited Focus on Test-Taking and Practical Skills

The theory overlooks important teaching aspects such as test-taking strategies, which may be crucial for adult learners' success. Similarly, it does not address how adult learners can develop practical skills for applying what they have learned in real-life scenarios, such as career advancement or personal growth.

Implications: Applying the Theory of Margin in Practice

To foster a supportive learning environment, consider the following steps:

1. Remove barriers and obstacles that hinder learning.

Identify external factors like time constraints, financial stress, transportation issues, or family responsibilities that may limit learners' capacity to engage in education. Offering flexible deadlines, asynchronous learning options, or free resources can ease financial burden on learners.

2. Provide learners with adequate resources and support.

Offer learners access to tutoring, counseling, study groups, online forums, and free materials to foster collaboration and peer support to keep them motivated.

3. Provide institutional support.

Advocate for policies that support adult learners, such as access to academic advising, career services, childcare, transportation, or mental health resources. As educators, we can also connect learners with community programs that offer financial aid, childcare, or transportation assistance.

4. Help students develop productive habits.

Teach your learners how to prioritize tasks using planners or digital tools. Encourage them to reflect through journaling or goal-setting exercises, so they know how to track their progress and adjust their learning strategies accordingly.

5. **Empathize with learners.**

Create a safe, nonjudgmental learning environment where learners feel comfortable discussing challenges. Use flexible teaching approaches, such as providing multiple ways to complete assignments to accommodate different needs and preferences.

The Theory of Transformative Learning

Jack Mezirow proposed **transformative learning**, a theory that suggests adults learn by critically reflecting on their beliefs, assumptions, and perspectives, which leads to meaningful learning. Transformative learning goes beyond acquiring new information. It involves fundamentally changing how individuals see themselves and their world, which leads them to make more informed decisions.

Limitations of Transformative Learning

While transformative learning provides a powerful framework for adult education, it has certain limitations:

1. **Time-Intensive Process**

True transformation requires time for reflection, discussion, and application. It's a lengthy, *complex process* that may not align with adult education timelines or suit learners, especially those with limited time for deep reflection.

2. **Emphasis on Critical Reflection**

The theory heavily focuses on *critical reflection* and overlooks the role of emotions, intuition, and social interactions, which are also crucial in the learning process. Emotions influence motivation and engagement; intuition can lead to meaningful insights, and social interactions help shape new perspectives. By prioritizing reflection, the theory may not fully capture the complexity of adult learning.

3. **Emotional Resistance**

Adults may feel defensive or uncomfortable when their beliefs are challenged, leading to resistance rather than transformation.

4. **Variability in Readiness**

Not all learners are open to transformative experiences; some may prefer straightforward, skill-based learning over deep self-examination.

5. **Lack of Practical Application**

The theory emphasizes perspective shifts but does not always provide clear strategies for applying new insights to real-world situations.

6. **Difficulty in Measuring Transformation**

Measuring whether a transformation has occurred can be difficult, as the process is *subjective* and often personal.

> Unlike traditional learning outcomes, which can be assessed through tests or observable skills, transformative learning involves changes in perspective that may not be easily quantified.

Implications: Applying Transformative Learning in Practice

To incorporate transformative learning in adult education, educators can:

1. **Promote critical thinking skills.**

Use methods like journaling, guided discussions, case studies, role-playing, and perspective-taking exercises. For example, in a GED, CTE, or HiSET math class focused on budgeting, you could have students track their monthly expenses, analyze case studies of people managing budgets, and reflect on how their personal financial habits align with their values and goals.

2. **Create safe learning environments.**

Build a classroom atmosphere that is supportive and open to diverse perspectives. Learners need to feel safe to share their thoughts and make mistakes as they explore new ways of thinking and learning. As teachers, we can model vulnerability by sharing our own experiences and promoting group discussions that respect diverse viewpoints.

3. **Facilitate discussions and peer learning.**

Create opportunities for learners to reflect on their experiences, assumptions, and beliefs. You can have structured debates, group discussions, and storytelling to encourage students to share and critically examine diverse perspectives.

4. Connect learning to real-life situations.

Use real-world experiences and problem-solving activities to connect theory to practice. Simulations, role-plays, case studies, and community projects help learners apply new knowledge, question preconceptions, and develop new perspectives based on hands-on experience.

Recognize that transformation does not happen overnight, so providing opportunities for ongoing reflection and learning is important. By engaging adult learners in critical reflection and challenging their assumptions, we can encourage deeper growth and knowledge retention.

How can these theories help you improve student retention?

These theories provide frameworks that you can use to create your own systems and environments that address the unique needs and challenges of your learners. Leveraging these theories leaves nothing to chance. A solid understanding of these concepts empowers you to make evidence-based calculated decisions to engage, motivate, equip, and support your learners. In Chapter 3, we'll explore how you can take matters into your own hands and start establishing your own student retention systems.

CHAPTER 3

Taking Matters into Your Own Hands

Do not follow where the path may lead. Go instead where there is no path and leave a trail.

– Ralph Waldo Emerson

If your program currently lacks a clear student retention system, don't worry—you can create one for your classroom. Having a system that works is the first step in keeping your learners engaged and supported.

When it comes to student retention, program administrators' influence is limited. You're the one who sees learners' challenges up close and understands their needs best. So, this gives YOU the opportunity to come in to save the day (or the semester!). It's up to you to make your classroom a place where students feel valued, motivated, and encouraged to persist.

Remember, for your learners, you're the ultimate learning guide, facilitator, and leader. Why do I say that? Because you shape their classroom and learning experience. As a result, most learners might decide to stay in class because of what you do, the support you offer—and how you make them feel inspired. The environment you create, the way you interact, and the encouragement you provide all matter. The key question is this: Do you have a system that focuses on your learners' needs?

However, let's be frank: it won't be easy. I know you want to do it for the sake of your learners, but how? You can start by telling them the truth.

A good system should enable you to give your learners *more* than they think they need. Give them **transferable skills, structure, agency, critical thinking, connections,** and—above all—a sense of **community** and **inspiration**.

The Lies That Stand in the Way

> All of the great leaders have had one characteristic in common: it was the willingness to confront unequivocally the major anxiety of their people in their time. This, and not much else, is the essence of leadership.
>
> — John Kenneth Galbraith

Most of your learners are afraid of failure, blame, and criticism. Can you recognize their fear? Unless you're well aware of their fear, you won't be able to help them "dance" with it. What do I mean?

Think of ballroom dancing. At first, you hesitate—you're afraid of stepping on toes, making mistakes, and looking foolish. But with time and practice, you gain confidence and start moving freely. The same applies with learning. Your students need to embrace their fears so they can grow. This might be the most important skill you ever teach.

Now, here's the truth: Adult learners often carry around lies they've been told about their learning abilities that perpetuate these fears. Let's imagine a student named Joanne who rarely speaks in class. Joanne is convinced she's not smart enough to keep up and worries her classmates will think she's stupid. Her teacher, Mr. Patel, notices that and starts calling on her for simple, low-risk questions. He pairs her with supportive classmates to gradually increase her participation. Over time, Joanne gains confidence—she asks questions, shares ideas, and even assists her peers. The lie that she wasn't "smart enough" no longer controls her.

We've all had students like Joanne who are held back by false beliefs about intelligence, success, and their abilities. As adult ed professionals, we have a responsibility to address these misconceptions and foster a growth mindset. In other words, we should help our students understand that intelligence isn't a fixed trait, mistakes are part of learning, and dedicated effort leads to improvement.

Let's tackle some common lies, one by one:

Lie #1: You can raise your hand only if you have the correct answer or something smart to say.

Reaction: As Seth Godin puts it, "It's OK to be wrong on the way to being right."

Lie #2: Don't ask stupid questions.

Reaction: See Lie #1!

Lie #3: Students who complete their work quickly are smart.

Reaction: When it comes to learning, the process is just as important as the outcome. Learning takes time and should not be rushed—this isn't the Olympic Games!

Lie #4: Don't speak if you don't know what you're talking about.

Reaction: This is misleading because students won't know if they are wrong unless they share their ideas.

Lie #5: You should get everything right the first time (if you're smart).

Reaction: Learning takes time and practice. Struggling at first doesn't mean you're not smart—it means you're learning. Even experts make mistakes before mastering a skill.

Lie #6: STEM is not for everyone.

Reaction: Really, who has the right to say that? Students just need a teacher who can open their eyes and minds to the STEM world. Anyone can learn whatever they want as long as they are willing to put in the work and the effort.

Lie #7: Having good grades means you're smart.

Reaction: In the marketplace, everything comes down to skills and competencies. Employers increasingly prioritize tangible skills, critical thinking, and problem-solving over academic grades

Lie #8: Students with high test scores are smart.

Reaction: See point # 7. As noted educator Dr. Carol Dweck puts it, "Test scores and measures of achievement tell you where a student is, but they don't tell you where a student could end up."

Lie #9: If you don't have a high IQ, you're not smart.

Reaction: The IQ test is just one way to measure intelligence. For example, most people would agree Albert Einstein had a very high IQ and was a genius. But most people fail to recognize that Einstein studied a lot and put in tremendous effort to accomplish what he did and published 450 papers. Success comes from effort, not just innate ability.

Lie #10: You need to go with the flow. Do your best to fit in.

Reaction: Fitting in is a guaranteed way to be invisible and fail in the marketplace.

Lie #11: If it's not on the test, it's not important, so don't worry about it.

Reaction: Students SHOULD worry about it. Their education should prepare them for the real world, not just for a test. Learning never stops. The real world is far bigger than any standardized exam.

Addressing these lies sends a clear message that adult education isn't about judgment, passing exams, or perfection—it's about creating a space where learners are free to grow, make mistakes, and improve day by day.

The Shame-Proof Classroom

Shame is a bad feeling. Nobody likes it. And learners won't keep coming back to a classroom where they experience shame and embarrassment.

> I've learned that people will forget what you said, people will forget what you did, but people will never forget how you made them feel.
>
> **– Maya Angelou**

To truly help adult learners thrive, we need to create a space that's free from judgment—a space that's welcoming and conducive to real-world learning. Your ability to create this mistake-friendly environment where learners can thrive is indispensable to their learning success.

A Balanced Approach To Learner Persistence

A balanced approach is most effective for optimal retention. This means combining both mechanical strategies and psychological solutions. Let's break this down:

> Good teaching cannot be reduced to technique; good teaching comes from the identity and integrity of the teacher.
>
> **– Parker Palmer**

Psychological Solutions focuses on the mental and emotional processes that influence retention. They emphasize motivation, mindset, and cognitive strategies that enhance learning. Students need to believe in their ability to succeed and view mistakes as part of the learning process. A positive mindset helps them to persevere through challenges.

Mechanical solutions provide structure and external tools to assist students in staying organized and consistent. Examples include using schedules, providing structured learning materials, and setting measurable goals. The theory of margin suggests that learners who are overloaded cannot effectively absorb the information. These strategies create a sense of order, making it easier for students to track progress and stay on track.

In other words, while mechanical solutions offer structure and clarity, psychological solutions address internal barriers like self-doubt and fixed mindsets. Together, these strategies create an environment where learners not only have the tools to succeed but are also mentally prepared to persist despite obstacles.

How can you create an environment that helps students overcome their fears and build the confidence to succeed in their learning?

As an educator, you have the power to influence retention through your actions, attitudes, and teaching strategies. By addressing the lies and misconceptions that hold learners back, fostering a classroom free of shame, and implementing both psychological and mechanical strategies, you can cultivate an atmosphere where learners thrive. Recognize each student's potential and empower them to keep coming back, day after day.

As we go onto Chapter 4, we'll explore how to identify the warning signs that a learner might be on the verge of giving up and how to support them before it's too late.

CHAPTER 4

Identifying the Warning Signs

A leader is one who sees more than others see, who sees farther than others see, and who sees before others see.

– Leroy Eimes

We put in the effort to motivate our students, build engagement, and create a supportive environment. But what if, despite our best efforts, we still see signs that some learners are about to give up and walk away?

An adult learner doesn't suddenly ditch a class (e.g., HiSET, GED, ASE, ABE, ESL/ELL, or Workforce) without warning. Instead, they gradually make this decision. Recognizing the warning signs of someone who's about to drop out allows you to reach out to these learners and offer **just-in-time support**. Timely intervention could potentially influence their decision.

But how do you show them you really care? First, by paying attention to the signs that indicate they are disengaging, either consciously or subconsciously. Let's examine the key warning signs and what you can do to address them.

> The reality is that most adult learners hesitate before giving up on a teacher who cares about them.

1. Frequent Unexcused Absences

Frequent absences often stem from learners struggling to keep up due to a heavy load, as explained by the theory of margin. Learners are more likely to disengage when the gap between their resources (time, energy, support) and the demands of the learning environment becomes too wide. This could leave them feeling like they'll never catch up with their classmates, resulting in the shame and frustration I mentioned earlier that can eventually lead to quitting.

What to Do:

- Reach out early to learners with many absences. Let them know you care and you're concerned about their learning.

- Offer practical assistance, but only in areas you can actually help with.

- Review expectations and provide extra support as needed.

- Assist them in leaving the class smoothly, so they can come back later if they like.

- Avoid making them feel judged.

It's critical to let students know you understand their situation and want to help them get back on track.

2. Constant Cell Phone Use

Learners who are constantly on the phone talking and texting during class might have other commitments (or distractions). It's often a sign they are mentally checked out. Some may feel guilty for breaking classroom rules, which can lead to disengagement.

What to Do:

- Have a conversation about the issue but don't come across as accusatory or condemning.

- Review class expectations together.

- Discuss potential solutions to the issues and provide accommodation as necessary.

- Help students in exiting the class gracefully if they truly need to, so they can return at a later time if they are able to.

3. Lack of Participation and Engagement

This is a crucial one. When learners stop asking questions, contributing to discussions, or engaging in activities, they are likely losing interest—or confidence. When learners are not involved in the learning process, they won't retain the information taught in class.

From an andragogical perspective, adult learners are self-directed, so disengagement often happens when the material doesn't connect to their personal goals, past experiences, or current needs.

What to Do:

- Address disengagement directly at the end of the class. You can try something like, "I've noticed you've been quiet lately. What's on your mind?"

- Get to know learners and connect lessons to their goals and interests.

- Develop and facilitate a variety of interactive activities like pair work, group discussions, and hands-on tasks to keep students involved.

- Minimize downtime. Long gaps in learning kill momentum and motivation.

- Encourage reflection at the end of every class so learners can track their progress and growth, allowing transformative learning to take place.

- Discuss students' work and progress biweekly or monthly and provide feedback and encouragement.

- Allow the space and time for all learners to think, reflect, and collaborate.

What to do:

I'll address the issue of learners' lack of engagement in more detail in Chapters 5 and 6.

4. No Personal Connection

Learners who feel isolated are at higher risk of walking away. Without any connections in the classroom or friends around, they may struggle to take risks, express their needs, and ask for help. In other words, they feel too vulnerable.

> This idea of shared humanity and the connections that we make with one another—that's what, in fact, makes life worth living.
>
> – Clint Smith

Understanding Maslow's hierarchy of needs can help you see why personal connection is an important factor in motivating your learners. I strongly encourage you to read more about this hierarchy.

What to Do:

- Foster a classroom community. Give students shared responsibilities and encourage teamwork.

- Create activities that build and reinforce the community structure, especially at the beginning of the class term. These can be icebreakers and team-building exercises.

- Get to know your learners. Understand what motivates them and what challenges they face.

- Encourage learners to work and study together in groups.

- Check on students both in groups and individually on a regular basis and listen to their concerns.

- Be intentional about providing time and space for learners to socialize during the semester.

- Implement group work and small group projects from day one.

Above all, learners need to know they can trust you. Many of our learners face personal, financial, or emotional struggles that can impact their learning. Recognizing what adult learners are going through is just as vital as teaching the material. My advice to you: don't miss or ignore the warning signs of a student struggling to attend the class. Keep an open line of communication and treat your learners with the utmost respect and consideration.

> You never know—you may just be the only motivation your learners have to attend classes regularly.

In Chapter 5, I'll guide you through different strategies you can use to create your own system—one that not only supports your learners but also fosters a classroom environment that keeps them engaged and eager to return.

CHAPTER 5

Building a System for Student Engagement and Retention

A good objective of leadership is to help those who are doing poorly to do well and to help those who are doing well to do even better.

– Jim Rohn

When it comes to learner retention, simply setting goals isn't enough. Goals alone rarely work. Shocking, right? What you need is to establish a system that supports learners in every step of their journey. You need a system that:

- Builds community.
- Encourages learners to build connections.
- Empowers learners to express their thoughts.
- Creates a safe environment for learners
- Gives them a desire to learn.
- Focuses on transferable skills.

Additionally, learners need to be taught how to build their own systems. For example, they need a system that helps them:

- Attend class regularly and on time.
- Study or work with classmates.
- Practice independently.

- Maintain balance in all aspects of their lives.

According to author and cartoonist Scott Adams, a system is better than a bunch of goals.

The Power of Systems: Why They Matter

Losing learners week after week is demoralizing for both you and the rest of your class. But things can get even worse. How?

The more learners you lose, the higher the risk of losing more. This creates a domino effect, which is why you must stop this trend early!

Keeping adult learners interested in your class requires more than teaching content—it takes a holistic approach. And trust me, I've been there. I personally find it difficult to keep all my learners interested. But I've never given up on a student!

Consider this: In your classroom, a learner named Julian struggles with time management. His work schedule is erratic, and he often misses class. But when you build a system where he feels supported, included, and empowered, his commitment to learning increases. By introducing weekly check-ins, study groups, and clear expectations, Julian can catch up by getting notes from classmates and managing his studies better. He begins to feel like part of a community, which motivates him to keep coming back.

Over the years, I've developed a system for my classes and coaching work that maximizes student engagement and retention. Let's review some interventions you can add to your system, regardless of the subject you teach.

Creating Your Own System

1. Raise awareness about why your class is important.

Your learners may not always know why they should study your content, so it's your responsibility to pitch your subject to them. List the specific skills they'll develop and how they can apply them in real-life situations. For example, instead of simply saying, "Math is useful," show them how it applies to budgeting, managing bills, construction work, or calculating overtime pay.

Use **stories, concrete examples, visuals**, and your **sense of humor** to get and keep the students' attention. Don't be too formal, plain, and boring. Instead, be approachable and relatable—after all, this is adult education!

At the end of the day, we have to give our learners a reason to trust us, study the content we present, and return to our classes.

2. Create a classroom community.

Forget about teaching for a moment and focus on building community. Encourage connections by incorporating get-to-know-you activities so you can learn about your students, and they can learn about each other. Small efforts, like learning their names, listening to their stories, checking in on their progress, and showing genuine interest in their lives, go a long way.

> "Setting the emotional climate for learning may be the most important task a teacher embarks on each day."
>
> – Dr. Mariale M. Hardiman

Create space for learners to mingle with each other and share their challenges, fears, expectations, and goals. In face-to-face settings, this can be as simple as small-group meetups or peer check-ins. For hybrid and online learners, foster engagement through virtual breakout rooms, discussion boards, collaborative digital spaces, and regular video check-ins.

This may take time, but it gives learners a sense of belonging (here we go again with Maslow's hierarchy of needs!). You never know—this sense of belonging might be the very thing that prevents your learners from giving up.

3. Teach time management.

Adult learners often struggle with balancing school, work, and family responsibilities, leading to inconsistent attendance or unfinished assignments. Developing a system that fits their lifestyle will help address those concerns.

Regardless of the focus of your course, teaching or reviewing effective time management strategies is critical to your learners' success. Here are some ways to address this:

- Have a conversation about the benefits of keeping a planner or digital calendar to track deadlines, class schedules, and study time.

- Share time management tools like templates, time-blocking methods, or smartphone apps that can help learners plan their daily and weekly schedules.

- Help students develop a schedule for the whole class term, factoring in major deadlines, personal obligations, and study time.

- Show learners how to identify urgent vs. important tasks and make realistic to-do lists.

- Encourage learners to block out time to study, read, and practice to build consistency.

Additionally, consider encouraging learners to study or work with friends, classmates, or family members who will hold them accountable. Having someone checking in can help motivate them to stay on track.

4. Keep an open line of communication.

Establish a communication system for your class so learners know what's expected and feel comfortable reaching out. Keep your system simple, consistent, and user-friendly.

> "Communication is the most important skill any leader can possess."
>
> **– Richard Branson**

Here's how:

- Set clear communication expectations. Discuss how learners should notify you about absences, lateness, or any issues affecting their attendance.

- Have students contribute to a notification policy for absences and tardiness.

- Set up and send out group reminders as necessary via text, Google Voice, or email.

- Discuss attendance policy and expectations with your class, such as the minimum hours required to take their post-test.

- Provide learners with tools to help them keep track of their attendance, if necessary. These can be sign-in sheets, attendance apps, or digital check-ins.

- Use group texts, calls (Google Voice), emails, and other relevant media to keep learners informed and connected.

- Reach out when learners miss class. A quick check-in shows that their presence matters and is noticeable.

- When reaching out to learners who are absent, use a friendly and understanding approach—never judgmental—to encourage their return.

- Use a well-structured communication system to foster good rapport with your class. The more learners feel heard and valued, the more likely they are to stay engaged in your class.

5. **Establish clear classroom routines.**

Take the guesswork out of your classroom setting. Be predictable. Establishing routines and a structured learning environment will make a difference.

Learners excel when they know what to expect, what actions to take, and how to find the materials they need.

Here's how:

- Outline clear performance objectives or goals for the class so that learners understand what they're working toward.

- Provide a detailed syllabus for the class term and go over it with your students. Invite them to make suggestions.

- Start and end your class on time.

- Be intentional when starting and closing your lesson. Ensure students leave with a sense of closure and key takeaways.

- Have a clear agenda that the class can refer to from time to time during lesson implementation and get your learners' input on when they feel ready to move forward.

- Show clear transitions from one unit to the next.

- Teach learners to organize their work and your handouts, whether through physical folders, digital binders, or online platforms.

- Give homework regularly if appropriate for your teaching context. This will encourage learners to review and practice course materials.

- Have a clear strategy in place to bring absentees up to speed. You can make it easier for them to catch up by providing notes, recorded lessons, or summary updates.

A solid structure or system will help learners develop productive study and work habits. However, be mindful that some learners may need extra support, so be prepared to customize your strategies and routines.

In the next chapter, I'll focus on how to improve our teaching by creating engaging, student-centered lessons that keep learners motivated.

CHAPTER 6

Raising Your Learning-Facilitation Game

For most of us, the problem isn't that we aim too high and fail—it's just the opposite—we aim too low and succeed.

– Sir Ken Robinson

No matter what you teach—math, science, social studies, CTE, ITE, ESL/ELL, or RELA—your learner retention rate will, for the most part, depend on the learning experience you offer your students.

Like me, you've probably had many teachers in your lifetime. But how many of their classes would you be happy to attend again if given the chance? I'm sure you wouldn't want to sit through any of the dreadful, dull ones.

Similarly, have you ever wondered how your learners feel about your classes? Would they choose to stay with you if other options are available?

Let's explore a few teaching techniques that can be critical to keeping learners engaged in the learning process—and committed to your classes.

1. **Create an active learning experience.**

Have you ever heard of **LX**? It stands for **"learner experience"** and is a big deal in the corporate world and academia. A strong LX taps into students' thoughts, emotions, and real-world experiences, making learning more meaningful and effective.

Adapting the principles of the LX into your adult ed classroom is great teaching practice. It works.

As a result, your teaching practices should tap into learners' minds, brains, and emotions to create a learning environment they want to return to.

No matter what you teach, how your learners feel in your classroom will shape their retention and success.

Here's how you can elevate your learners' experience:

Create an active learning experience.

- Create opportunities for students to respond, manipulate, and react to class content. Encourage them to bring examples and their own personal experiences into the lessons.

- Give learners a voice and encourage them to use it. This helps activate their prior knowledge and deepens understanding.

- "Storify" your content by presenting your content in the form of stories and create space for learners to interact with the stories.

- Use real-life scenarios, concrete examples, and discussions that mimic reality—especially your learners' reality.

- Differentiate your instructions by aligning your content with learners' diverse needs and interests.

- Develop learners' transferable skills, like critical thinking, group work, public speaking, note-taking, and reading comprehension. Encourage them to apply the learning in their context right away.

- Apply good classroom management techniques to establish a secure and productive learning environment that makes students take more risks.

- Help students reflect on their learning and understand how their learning connects to broader goals.

- Have regular conversations about what's working well in the class and what needs to be changed or adjusted.

2. **Teach how to learn, unlearn, and relearn.**

Students who use **metacognitive skills**—that is, understand how they learn and use techniques to enhance their learning—are way ahead of the game.

Ask yourself: What's your teacher talk time vs. student talk time? If you're doing most of the talking, you may be handing them answers instead of guiding them on

> "The illiterate of the 21st century will not be those who can-not read and write, but those who cannot learn, unlearn, and relearn."
>
> – Alvin Toffler

how to find them. It's the difference between giving them a fish and teaching them how to fish.

Teaching students how to learn is empowering and sets them on the path to autonomy. How do you do that?

Here are some ways:

- Show learners how to access and organize information for study.
- Teach study skills, strategies, and the best ways to handle class content.
- Use **active questioning**—let learners generate and respond to guiding questions.
- Keep learners on task and challenge their assumptions.
- Flip the class, if possible, encouraging students to review content before coming to class and providing independent study time or review time.
- Implement pair work and group work as often as possible to promote peer learning.
- Use guiding and follow-up questions and let learners do the same.
- Create room for debates and discussions. This will allow learners to articulate and clarify their thoughts and opinions.
- Encourage learners to produce tangible and meaningful outcomes while effectively managing their learning tasks.
- Support learners in connecting new knowledge to prior knowledge through discussions, visuals, and scaffolding.
- Use guidelines and frameworks, such as the following:
  - Universal Design for Learning (UDL)

- Brain-Targeted Teaching Model (BTT)
- Presentation–Practice–Production/Use (PPP/U)
- Pre-During-Post (PDP) for Reading or Listening
- 5E Model (Engage, Explore, Explain, Elaborate, and Evaluate)
- SQ3R (Survey, Question, Read, Recite, and Review) Reading Method
- KNOWS Method (Know, Need to Know, Organize, Work, and Solution) for math problem-solving

These tools have facilitated my teaching work and made my instructional coaching job easier. They offer step-by-step guidance for lesson planning and delivery.

3. **Celebrate effort over talent.**

"Hard work beats talent when talent fails to work hard."

– Kevin Durant

Talent is overrated. Let's face it, many adult learners have struggled with low self-esteem at some point. Previous negative learning experiences may have prevented them from performing at their best before they started taking your class. This is where you come in to elevate them! Shifting the focus from being smart to being hard-working will encourage students to step up and do more.

Having a conversation about the superiority of hard work over talent is critical to a learner's success. In other words, do your best to give feedback when learners show effort, determination, resilience, and tenacity.

Make sure that even the smallest progress is acknowledged, and provide constructive, corrective feedback so they can fix their mistakes and improve their work. And don't forget to applaud learners for having the courage to try, even when they make mistakes.

How can you do that? Here are some ways:

- Welcome mistakes and leverage them as valuable opportunities to help learners improve their skills. Rather than focusing only on finding the right answers, emphasize the importance of the process.

- Provide specific feedback on completed tasks. Praise efforts.

- Encourage learners to keep a portfolio—a collection of works or achievements—so they can monitor and see their improvement.

- Celebrate instances of leadership and responsibility.

- Acknowledge and commend good time-management efforts.

- Praise decision-making skills and critical thinking.

- Value collaborative skills and teamwork.

- Encourage group work skills.

- Celebrate a positive outlook and attitude.
- Conduct regular check-ins with learners, and address challenges or concerns that might stand in the way.

The bottom line is to create positive learning experiences that elevate and empower your learners.

4. **Build factual knowledge for critical thinking.**

> Research in cognitive science shows that our brains naturally avoid complex thinking unless conditions are optimized. Daniel Willingham, cognitive scientist and author, explains it best:
>
> "The very processes that teachers care about most—critical thinking, reasoning, and problem-solving—are intimately intertwined with factual knowledge stored in long-term memory."
>
> **(Willingham, 2009, p. 22)**

It's common to hear that we should prioritize critical thinking in education. But here's the catch: students can't think critically without a strong foundation of factual knowledge.

That is to say, your students will learn and think better if they have some background knowledge about the content or subject you teach. If a task is too difficult and provides no sense of progress, students will feel frustrated. But if a task is too easy, it lacks challenge and engagement. I'd suggest **cognitive tasks** that introduce new challenges by building on what students already know how to do:

- Activate prior knowledge using videos, discussions, or storytelling before introducing key content.

- Pre-teach important concepts or vocabulary to help students access and engage with the content.

- Use thought-provoking questions that encourage students to express their personal opinions.

- Design tasks that challenge without overwhelming students.

5. Leverage learners' curiosity.

During my closing statement at a workshop on improving the quality of adult teaching, I made this statement: "Finding the correct answer, answering obvious questions, filling in the blanks are all boring activities—and stand in the way of effective student learning."

A participant quickly raised her hand and asked, "How about the tests? Don't we have to prepare our learners for these tests?"

I liked the question. It's a classic one that I often get when I discuss using engaging teaching practices in adult education. So, I explained my perspective.

While it's obvious adult learners want to succeed on these tests, they aren't thrilled with the questions themselves.

I have yet to meet an adult student who is dying to take a standardized test because the content and the questions were so interesting.

It's true that helping learners ace a test is crucial. However, preparing students for the test in a traditional worksheet-heavy manner can easily lead to boredom and disengagement. When learners tune out, they're less likely to perform well.

But the most important thing I said was this: We can prepare students for tests while keeping them interested in the learning process. How? By tapping into their curiosity. Why is that necessary? Let me explain…

Adult students might not like to think critically because it's hard. But they are all curious. How do I know? It's human nature! For instance, the cognitive scientist, Dr. Daniel Willingham, put it this way: "People are naturally curious, but we are not naturally good thinkers; unless the cognitive conditions are right, we will avoid thinking."

Here are some ways you can tap into your learners' curiosity:

- **Avoid obvious, closed-ended questions.** Use open-ended questions that invite deeper exploration.

- **Introduce an element of surprise**. Present information in a way that makes students want to know more.

- **Encourage inquiry-based learning**. Let students formulate and investigate their own questions.

- **Implement real-world connections** that make learning feel relevant and exciting.

- **Use multimedia-rich content in online settings**. Videos, interactive simulations, and virtual field trips can increase curiosity and engagement.

Learners have the desire to understand, try, and seek out what's coming next—but this desire needs to be activated. Once they get a taste of what's ahead, their eagerness grows. Imagine having a group of students who can't wait to start the next lesson.

6. Make storytelling work for you.

> "The human mind seems exquisitely tuned to understand and remember stories."
>
> **– Daniel Willingham**

From the beginning of time, storytelling has captured the imaginations of humans. The secret to teaching classes that learners will comprehend and remember is to organize the whole lesson—from beginning to end—like a good story. For example, structuring your lesson like a story should be like creating an episode of a popular TV show—it's got to be engaging, thought-provoking, and memorable. In other words, embed important concepts, key information, and instructions in well-crafted narratives to make learning intriguing and unforgettable.

You might be wondering, "How do I organize my lesson like a story?" Great question. Let's get to it now. A compelling story has the following ingredients:

1. **Causality:** Events should connect logically, leading from one idea to the next.

2. **Conflict:** Introduce a challenge or problem that sparks curiosity.

3. **Complication:** Add twists that require deeper thinking or problem-solving.

4. **Characters:** Create relatable situations or personas to bring concepts to life.

5. **Action:** Make learning active by incorporating movement, discussions, or real-world applications.

6. **The And-But-Therefore Formula:** Structure lessons with a logical flow:

   - AND (introduce key ideas)

   - BUT (introduce a challenge or contradiction)

   - THEREFORE (present solutions or insights)

Whether you teach in a traditional, online, or hybrid classroom, your role is to make learners feel curious, supported, and empowered to learn. By focusing on these strategies, you can raise your learning-facilitation game and transform your students' educational journey.

> A great teacher doesn't just deliver content—they create an engaging, meaningful learning experience.

In the next chapter, we'll shift our focus to fostering deeper learning by helping students develop **flexible knowledge** and **transferable skills**—essential for real-world success.

CHAPTER 7

Flexible Knowledge and Transferable Skills

> The gardener does not make a plant grow. The job of a gardener is to create optimal conditions.
>
> – Sir Ken Robinson

Now that you've retained most of your learners, let's discuss how we can promote deeper learning. Remember, our calling in adult education is to prepare students for the real world, not just for compliance testing. To achieve this, we must ensure that our teaching creates learners who can apply their knowledge flexibly, think critically, and demonstrate transferable skills.

The question is this: What level of knowledge do you want learners to develop? Answering that question will enable you to choose your teaching activities carefully. Let's take a look at what I mean by levels of knowledge and how to move your students from basic understanding to a deeper, more flexible application of their skills.

1. Rote Knowledge

Rote knowledge is superficial. It's about memorizing and repeating factual information. Therefore, learners might be able to use or repeat rote knowledge without understanding its meaning, implication, and application.

Don't let your students remain at this stage! Rather, take them to the next level. Take learning deeper and make learners work on meaningful learning tasks.

2. Inflexible Knowledge

New knowledge is inflexible and volatile. It's not effective learning, but it's better than rote knowledge. Think of it like a first runner-up in a spelling bee: it's better, but not the very best.

According to cognitive scientist Dr. Daniel Willingham, inflexible knowledge is a level of learning that allows students to perform tasks only in known contexts or settings where the knowledge was learned. It's not deep enough to be transferred to other contexts. Again, we still need to reinforce this kind of learning.

How? By using **distributed practice activities**—such as spaced repetition, real-world problem-solving tasks, and varied practice scenarios—that reflect the real world. These activities can enable your students to form *flexible* knowledge. What is flexible knowledge? Good question! The next section provides the answer.

3. Flexible Knowledge

Cognitive science research shows that flexible knowledge is a higher order of learning where students understand not just the facts, but also their meanings, implications, and applications. It's about developing critical thinking skills and learning how to transfer knowledge across different contexts, including testing.

In other words, this knowledge is transferable because it's rooted and based on what cognitive scientists call **deep-structure learning**. What do I mean by deep-structure learning? Allow me to explain.

Dr. Willingham defines deep structure as the ability to transfer learning and skills to various contexts. It's the ability to understand and use **abstract conceptualization**—the process of identifying underlying patterns and principles—and **generalization**—the ability to apply those principles to new and different situations. It encompasses critical thinking and problem-solving skills.

Reaching deep-structure learning can be challenging, but you can help students achieve it. How? By focusing on cognitive tasks, real-world examples, and experiences that allow students to transform inflexible learning into flexible knowledge. The more students do tasks that promote deep-structure learning, the better they will be at transferring their knowledge to different real-life situations.

For instance, several teaching approaches can lead to this level of learning, including case-based learning, project-based learning, problem-based learning, and experiential learning. Let's take a closer look at each of them.

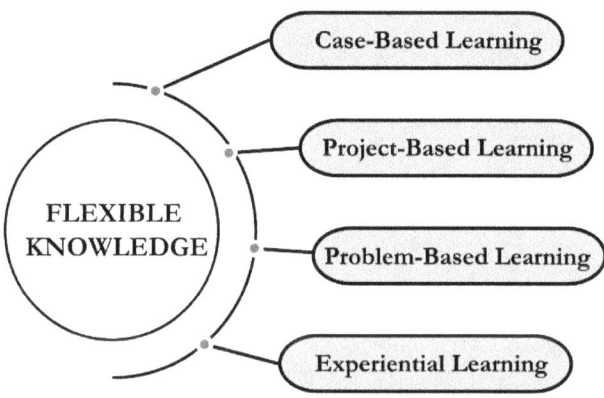

Figure 4: Teaching Approaches to Develop Flexible Knowledge

Teaching Approaches for Developing Flexible Knowledge

Case-Based Learning

Using this approach, adult ed instructors create opportunities for learners to use critical thinking and analytical skills while working on real-world challenges. By working in groups or pairs, students can delve into actual cases and analyze them from multiple perspectives.

Mastering CBL implementation might take time, but working on this skill is worth every minute you spend on it. You can develop your own case studies based on real-life experiences—whether from your own work, industry trends, or student experiences—or find existing ones in books, online resources, or professional training materials.

It's no exaggeration to say that becoming a proficient user of this approach will elevate you to the ranks of top learning facilitators in the adult ed field. Wouldn't you like that? Let's examine how to effectively apply this approach through a scenario.

Scenario:

Maria is working full-time at a retail store. She earns $3,000 per month before taxes. Her monthly expenses include:

- Rent: $1,200
- Utilities: $200
- Groceries: $500
- Childcare: $600
- Transportation: $250
- Miscellaneous: $250

Maria wants to start saving for emergencies and reduce her credit card debt, which has a balance of $1,500 with a 20% interest rate.

Task for Students:

- Analyse Maria's budget and identify areas where she can cut expenses.
- Calculate how much she could save per month by making adjustments.
- Compare different debt repayment strategies (minimum payments vs. paying extra).

- Discuss long-term financial planning strategies for stability.

This exercise mirrors the type of problem-solving required in the CASAS Life and Work Reading and Math tests, as well as real-life financial decision-making skills needed in the workforce. It encourages critical thinking, applied math, and financial literacy—all essential for adult learners.

Project-Based Learning

Like Case-Based Learning, project-based learning activities mimic the real world. With this approach, students work over an extended period to solve complex problems or complete meaningful projects. This method encourages collaboration, creativity, and practical problem-solving.

Now you might be wondering: What kind of projects should your learners work on? They should do work aligned with the core standards and learning objectives they are trying to reach. Use PBL guidelines and frameworks to help learners demonstrate their understanding and skills in evidence. For example, having them showcase real products they create will boost their confidence and presentation skills.

Example:

In a workforce innovation program, students can develop a Workplace Safety Handbook for a specific industry, such as construction, healthcare, or manufacturing. This project requires them to research OSHA safety regulations, interview professionals in the field, and compile best practices into an easy-to-understand guide.

Throughout the project, students will:

- **Apply reading comprehension skills** by analyzing safety manuals and regulations.

- **Develop writing and editing skills** by organizing information into clear, structured sections.

- **Demonstrate numeracy skills** by including calculations for safe weight limits, temperature tolerances, or hazardous material handling.

- **Enhance digital literacy** by formatting their handbook using word-processing software or even designing an infographic for quick reference.

At the end of the project, students will have the chance to present their safety handbook to a panel of industry professionals or local business owners, reinforcing public speaking skills and real-world application.

Problem-Based Learning

The Problem-Based Learning model allows adult ed teachers to foster classroom collaboration, allowing learners to show critical thinking skills and creativity. In this approach, learners tackle open-ended problems that require the utilization of skills aligned with the learning objectives set for the class. Applying the PBL principles can set you apart as an instructor.

But I already know what you're thinking: How is problem-based learning different from project-based learning? Well, you're right. They're close cousins. Simply put, many consider problem-based learning as a subcategory of project-based learning. Problem-based learning can be implemented in a short period of time, while project-based learning calls for more resources and a more extended period of time.

The following is a scenario you can use to implement PBL in your classroom.

Scenario:

A local small business is seeking to reduce its environmental footprint. The business is trying to reduce waste, use more sustainable materials, and minimize energy consumption. Learners must assess the business's current practices and develop an **environmental sustainability plan** that aligns with the company's goals.

Skills Applied:

- **Environmental Science:**

    - Analyze the business's current practices and identify areas for improvement.

    - Research and apply sustainable business practices such as using eco-friendly packaging or reducing water and energy consumption.

- **Project Management and Budgeting:**

    - Create an action plan for implementing sustainability initiatives.

    - Develop a budget to implement the changes and assess long-term cost savings.

- **Writing and Communication:**

    - Write an environmental sustainability report for the business.

    - Present findings and recommendations to business owners or managers.

In this scenario, students will gain practical problem-solving skills by helping a business implement more sustainable practices while also learning about budgeting and project management.

Experiential Learning

This teaching approach is all about learning by doing and reflecting on experiences. Adult ed instructors often use it to expose learners to experiences outside the classroom setting. Doing this enables learners to actively engage in real-world activities and reflect on their experiences to deepen their understanding.

In this model, students move through a learning cycle that includes the following phases:

1. **Concrete Experience:** Learners engage in a hands-on activity or real-world experience.

2. **Reflective Observation:** After the experience, learners take time to reflect on what happened and how it felt.

3. **Abstract Conceptualization:** Learners connect their experience to theoretical concepts and frameworks they've learned about in class.

4. **Active Experimentation:** Learners apply what they've learned by testing out new ideas or strategies in future situations.

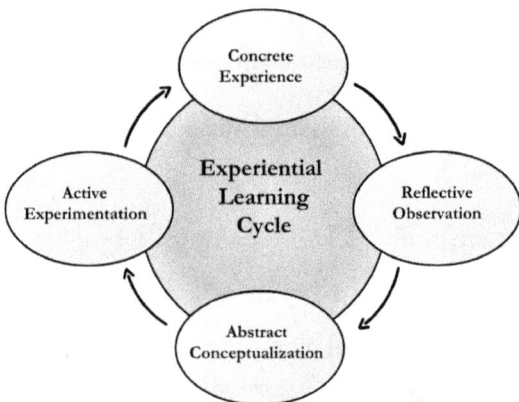

Figure 5: Kolb's Experiential Learning Theory

Example:

Imagine you're teaching a group of adult ESL/ELL learners who are working on everyday English and basic math skills, with a focus on understanding costs and budgeting.

Phase 1: Concrete Experience

You can organize a classroom activity where learners are given a list of items they might buy in a store, such as groceries or household goods. They will practice reading the items in English and calculating the total cost. This helps them practice both language and math skills at the same time.

Phase 2: Reflective Observation

After the activity, you ask the learners reflective questions, such as:

- "What English words or phrases did you use to ask for help with prices?"
- "How did you feel using English to ask for help or information?"
- "What was easy or difficult about reading the prices in English?"

Phase 3: Abstract Conceptualization

Next, you explain the math concepts behind budgeting, like adding up prices and calculating taxes in English. You also introduce key vocabulary for budgeting, such as "total," "discount," and "savings."

Phase 4: Active Experimentation

Finally, you challenge the learners to create a simple budget for their weekly shopping in English. They apply the skills they've learned by planning a budget using a list of items, adding prices, and calculating the total.

Through this process, learners not only practice language skills but also gain practical knowledge they can use in their everyday lives.

The bottom line is that being proficient in all four teaching approaches is ideal. However, mastering one approach can still be effective. Like I said before, facilitating learning like a pro is a win-win situation for you and your learners—they learn better and you look better (professionally).

A Note about Automaticity

Unfortunately, learners who struggle to master basic skills and information in the adult ed classroom usually have difficulty engaging in higher-order thinking and mental tasks. To reach deep-structure learning and complete mental tasks successfully, they must first reach **automaticity** in their use of basic skills, information, and procedures related to the content.

So, what can we do to promote automaticity in our students? We can plan regular, consistent, distributed practice sessions that enable students to work on foundational skills and procedures until they reach automaticity. Just as we use Case-Based Learning to encourage critical thinking and Project-Based Learning to foster creativity and problem-solving, students also need frequent, distributed

> As Dr. Willingham says, "Automaticity is vital in education because it allows us to become more skillful in mental tasks."

practice to solidify their basic skills. Reaching automaticity will ensure their success when dealing with more complex mental activities in and out of the adult ed classroom.

For example, your learners will do better if they've reached automaticity in:

- Solving math problems if they've mastered basic operations, the order of operations, and key mathematical concepts.

- Accessing scientific texts to recall basic factual knowledge and understanding key concepts or terminology.

- Reading different types of texts once they know how to read for comprehension (that is, being able to identify the main idea, details, the author's intent, and clues about context).

- Understanding common vocabulary, grammar rules, and language structures to better navigate tasks in a real-world context or in academic and professional settings.

By focusing on building automaticity, we prepare learners to excel in the more advanced activities promoted by case-based, project-based, and problem-based learning.

Allow me to quote Dr. Willingham once more to cement my point: "...procedures must be learned to the point of automaticity so that they no longer consume working memory space." In other words, when your students master basic skills to the point that they can apply them automatically—like knowing their multiplication table—they'll be able to think more clearly and quickly.

Now that we've established the importance of building deep and flexible knowledge, it's time to turn our attention to formal testing. Passing tests may not be the ultimate goal, but it's a reality. In the upcoming chapter, let's explore how to prepare our students for this critical game day.

CHAPTER 8

Test Preparation (Game Day!)

Language-lovers know that there is a word for every fear. Are you afraid of wine? Then you have oenophobia. Tremu-lous about train travel? You suffer from siderodromopho-bia. Having misgivings about your mother-in-law is pen-theraphobia, and being petrified of peanut butter sticking to the roof of your mouth is arachibutyrophobia. And then there's Franklin Delano Roosevelt's affliction, the fear of fear itself, or phobophobia.

– Steven Pinker

Testophobia is a common fear that affects many learners. Therefore, we must equip ourselves with evidence-based strategies to help our learners manage this fear.

I held off on writing about testing for a while because if your students can reach mastery or flexible knowledge, we think testing will take care of itself. But even with strong skills and knowledge, students need to learn to perform under pressure. So, are you ready to dive into the preparation tips for standardized testing? OK, then let's get started!

It's a fact that some of your learners might not perform well under testing pressure. This is why your class should start training on the very first day of class. Be sure to have your students practice under simulated test conditions at least every other week. By the time they take the final test, their brain will have gotten used to its intensity.

Covering key standards (Common Core, Next Generation Science Standards, EL Proficiency Standards, GED and HiSET Standards, NRS, TABE, CASAS, and College & Career Readiness) is vital, but it's insufficient to lead students to perform well on standardized tests. Why? Your students also need to know the **test instructions, timing,** and **structure**—and know them very well.

Unfortunately, learners who do not perform well on the tests might get discouraged and leave your class or program. This is demoralizing for both you and your learners, isn't it? But the good news is that you can almost always avoid this pitfall by thoughtful test preparation, mastery-focused teaching, and familiarizing students with the test format.

Here are a few useful ways to help students prepare for taking tests:

1. Write learner-centered learning objectives.

Set learning objectives (LOs) instead of coverage objectives (COs). COs are about the content you and your institution want to cover in the class. But we both know these COs won't necessarily lead to effective learning, right?

That's why writing LOs is the way to go. They indicate what skills and competencies your students should master by the end of your lesson. Your LOs should reflect real-world, authentic experiences, which helps students better connect their knowledge to the actual test. For example, instead of simply covering a reading passage in a lesson, you could focus on objectives like: "By the end of this lesson, students will be able to identify the main idea and supporting details of a passage." This approach encourages deeper, more meaningful learning, which is key to long-term retention and great test performance. As Dr. Willingham points out, "The brain stores most information in the form of meaning."

2. Distribute your practice sessions.

As I mentioned before, avoiding massed practices or cramming is key. Not only is making students practice lots of materials in a short period too cumbersome, but it doesn't foster long-term retention or improve performance on a test.

Rather, opting for **distributed practice**—spreading out your practice sessions as much as possible over several weeks—works better. For example, assign practice problems throughout the term, so students regularly revisit material and improve over time. This will also be an opportunity to recycle content and practice managing *testophobia* by using some mindfulness techniques.

The reason this method is effective lies in the concept of the **spacing effect**. In other words, the spacing effect will work in your and your students' favor. (Yes, the spacing effect is a thing!)

> Essentially, the more you space out practice sessions over time, the better prepared students will be when it's time for the test.

Now, let's briefly address the importance and benefits of practice. Practice is what exercise is for your body. As Dr. Willingham (2009) puts it, "It is virtually impossible to become proficient at a mental task without extended practice."

Simply put, practice (or guided learning) is helpful in numerous ways. For instance, it:

- Helps develop and reinforce new skills.
- Prevents us from forgetting recently learned information and skills.
- Facilitates knowledge transfer to long-term memory.
- Makes thinking processes automatic.
- Reinforces memory.
- Transforms surface knowledge into deep-structure learning.

From a cognitive science perspective, learners practice well when they are intentional in what they do. For example, they need to:

- Seek out and use constructive feedback to fix mistakes and improve skills.
- Concentrate on honing specific skills or understand how to effectively learn new skills.
- Reflect on their progress and decide how to move forward accordingly.

Effective feedback also motivates your learners. It acts like fuel that keeps their learning engine running and should encompass the following elements:

1. **Timely:** Feedback should be given soon after the work has been completed and still fresh in students' minds.
2. **Corrective:** It points to specific issues that need fixing and suggests how to improve the work.
3. **Criterion-based**: Learners are informed how they are doing in relation to a specific standard, goal, or rubric they are expected to meet.

4. **Student-facilitated:** It allows learners to have a voice in the process. They are given a chance to articulate their specific needs or weaknesses and request appropriate support.

If learners receive no feedback on their assignments, their attendance in class and the effort they put in can feel meaningless—like flying a plane without radar or guidance from the control tower. The bottom line is this: make effective feedback an integral part of all your practice sessions.

3. **Teach study skills and strategies for THE TEST.**

Using effective study skills makes learners more confident, and their confidence improves even more when they are consistent in their studies. For example, 30 minutes of study a day over 15 weeks is way better than 20 hours of study just before the final test. This is where the spacing effect comes into play—it strengthens memory retention and ensures better preparation when test day arrives.

At the heart of the approach is **repeated practice,** especially over extended periods. It's by far the best remedy against forgetfulness. To quote Dr. Willingham, "Anticipating the effect of forgetting dictates that we continue our practice beyond the mastery we desire" (Willingham, 2004).

Equally important, learners need to practice and connect new material with what they already know. Doing so strengthens memory pathways, leading to deeper comprehension and better retention of information. Isn't that what we all aim for?

Finally, good performance on standardized tests can boost learners' motivation. The better they do, the more they want to learn—and the more persistent they become about learning. And that's exactly what you and your adult ed program aspire to achieve.

Key Strategies for Test Preparation

1. **Focus on *big-picture thinking*.**

   Help students develop the skills to identify main ideas, key details, and connections between concepts. For example, when learning about fractions, show how they relate to percentages and decimals rather than treating them as isolated topics.

2. **Present the lesson in *story format*.**

   The brain is wired for storytelling. Instead of explaining historical events as a list of facts, frame them as narratives with characters, conflicts, and resolutions. For math, turn word problems into relatable scenarios, like planning a budget for a road trip. Use practice tests weekly to assess understanding and close comprehension gaps.

3. **Use weekly practice tests to assess understanding and close gaps.**

   Frequent low-stakes tests help identify weak areas early. For instance, if students consistently struggle with word problems, you can introduce targeted exercises to build confidence before the actual test.

4. **Don't mistake practice test performance for real learning.**
   Good performance on practice tests is no indicator that learners will do well on the actual test.

5. **Develop automaticity in fundamental skills.**

   Help students achieve *automaticity* in foundational skills, like reading, vocabulary, and the four basic operations in math. You can use quick drills or timed exercises to reinforce fluency.

6. **Encourage students to explain concepts in multiple formats.**

   Allow students to show their understanding of concepts and ideas orally, in writing, or through drawings, either to themselves or classmates.

7. **Teach self-testing and retrieval strategies.**

   Teach learners to test or quiz themselves by using retrieval strategies. They can use flashcards, write practice questions, or cover their notes and try to recall key points before checking their answers.

8. **Promote *meta-awareness*—attention to attention.**

   Assist students in recognizing when their focus drifts by developing strategies to refocus, such as using short breaks, mindfulness techniques, or active note-taking to stay engaged.

CHAPTER 9

Real-World Learning-Facilitation Guidelines

> Today's world needs a workforce of creative, curious, and self-directed lifelong learners who are capable of conceiving and implementing novel ideas. Unfortunately, this is the type of student that the Prussian model actively sup-presses.
>
> — Salman Khan

Throughout this book, I've been emphasizing the importance of real-world learning. But I know what you're thinking: "Facilitating real-world learning sounds hard!" Yes, it does. We can't just plan out our lessons on the back of a napkin after dinner and walk into class the next day expecting to make a difference. Facilitating real-world learning required a LOT of planning and work. But creating a learning experience that transforms our students' lives is imperative.

This is the emotional labor we signed up for, so we should follow through and keep our promises to our learners. As we discussed earlier in this book, our goal is to guide them to become better, one classroom session at a time.

> Transforming our students into lifelong learners with strong 21st-century skills is like climbing Mount Everest! But what other option do we have?

Since it's hard, maybe real-world learning-facilitation guidelines are a good place to start. They might help you prioritize cognitive tasks, metacognitive skills, and real-world examples and experiences. Coupled with the right tools and strategies, these learning-facilitation guidelines can assist students in transforming shallow learning into flexible knowledge.

The guidelines are divided into seven sections:

1. Real-Word Teaching Goals
2. Learner-Centered Facilitation
3. Decision-Making
4. Effective Classroom Practice
5. Learning Reinforcement
6. Assessment and Evaluation
7. Learning or Knowledge Transfer

You don't have to cover all the principles in these seven sections in every lesson you teach. But when you plan your module or lesson unit, keep these principles in mind. They can guide you in delivering instruction and creating learning tasks that mimic the real world.

Section I- Real-World Teaching Goals

1. Promote deep-structure learning, mastery, and learner autonomy.

2. Transfer classroom learning to real-world situations.

3. Encourage a growth mindset among students by protecting them against learning stereotypes and addressing self-esteem issues, such as negative past learning experiences that may prevent learners from doing their best.

4. Develop speaking or communication skills (regardless of the subject you teach).

5. Increase reading comprehension skills through summarizing and analyzing evidence.

6. Develop writing skills through structured tasks and peer review.

7. Promote students' critical thinking skills.

8. Increase technology skills by integrating digital tools and platforms into learning.

9. Develop emotional intelligence, self-regulation, and leadership skills.

Section II- Learning-Centered Facilitation ✓

1. Start with real-world questions that drive discussions, encouraging students to pose additional questions.

2. Pique learners' curiosity to deepen engagement and improve retention.

3. Use an inquiry-based approach and experiential learning to promote learning by doing and reflecting.

4. Make the learning process rigorous by challenging assumptions and making learners think on their feet.

5. Avoid giving answers out too freely; instead, motivate learners to search, discover, explore, while supporting their thoughts and ideas.

6. Leverage learners' passion and interest by allowing them freedom and space to personalize and individualize their assignments or projects.

7. Apply the most effective teaching modalities and provide diverse resources, like videos, demonstrations, texts, audios, authentic materials and real-life examples.

8. Foster asynchronous discussions to accommodate flexible schedules.

9. Create a safe and risk-free environment while helping learners acknowledge and deal with their fears.

10. Implement adaptive learning technologies that personalize learning by adjusting content based on students' progress.

11. Bring experts or other professionals into the class and encourage learners to ask questions.

12. Support peer-learning through online discussions and forums and encourage students to participate or moderate forums.

Section III- Decision-Making

1. Create space for learners to participate in decision-making and share their opinions, thoughts, and feelings.

2. Give learners time and space to contemplate how they best think, work, and learn (that is, to reflect on identifying key issues, make adjustments and request appropriate help).

3. Encourage students to create learning products that match their level of readiness, as well as their personal and career goals.

4. Facilitate online reflection by using tools like discussion boards or journals, for learners to reflect on their learning process and make adjustments.

5. Design collaborative activities where students analyze content, find meaning, and make decisions together to showcase their comprehension and skills.

6. Use virtual tools like online group discussions, peer feedback sessions, or collaborative projects to demonstrate comprehension and skills.

Section IV- Effective Classroom Practice

1. Teach how to learn or the best ways to access and practice your material by taking on the role of a mentor or a coach.

2. Build learners' background knowledge in your subject area. Ensure they can analyze, synthesize, and critique content.

3. Promote effective and consistent practice with intent and free of distractions.

4. Teach effective study techniques and the best ways to learn and master target content.

5. Implement activities that make learners think deeply about new material and skills.

6. Welcome mistakes and celebrate efforts and hard work.

7. Schedule practice sessions over several weeks to avoid massed practices or cramming.

8. Promote peer learning, teamwork, and discussions both in-person and online.

9. Avoid idle time and promote healthy breaks.

10. Provide asynchronous practice options for self-paced learning.

11. Use interactive online content, like videos, quizzes, and simulations.

12. Facilitate online peer reviews and feedback sessions.

Section V - Learning Reinforcement

1. Incorporate well-designed extension activities or projects that build on classroom skills.

2. Create opportunities for learners to engage in real-world challenges requiring critical thinking by using the case-based learning approach.

3. Implement project-based learning where students develop real-world solutions, creating products or presentations for a specific audience.

4. Use a problem-based learning model to foster classroom collaboration, allowing learners to show critical thinking skills and creativity

5. Provide in-person or virtual networking and mentorship opportunities to connect learning with real-world applications.

6. Leverage discussion forums or online peer reviews to extend learning beyond the classroom.

VI- Assessment and Evaluation ✓

1. Assess and evaluate students' learning with authentic assessment tools that simulate real-life contexts, such as case studies and real-world tasks.

2. Collect and use learners' performance data to make necessary adjustments.

3. Keep learners informed on their progress by using specific standards, goals, or rubrics.

4. Hold groups and individuals accountable using participation rubrics and guidelines.

5. Provide timely, corrective, and criterion-based feedback.

6. Use digital assessment tools (quizzes, polls, discussion boards, or interactive assignments) to monitor learner progress in real-time.

7. Leverage adaptive learning platforms that modify difficulty levels based on student performance for personalized assessment.

8. Use e-portfolios where students upload projects, reflections, and skill demonstrations.

9. Implement learning and assessment portfolios to track student progress over time.

10. Promote self-reflection by allocating time for students to assess their own learning.

11. Assess understanding through observed performance on tasks rather than asking, "Do you understand?"

VII- Knowledge Transfer

1. Create tasks for learners to apply knowledge learned in class to real-world situations.

2. Motivate learners to solve open-ended problems using creativity, critical thinking, and practical skills.

3. Expose learners to experiences outside the classroom setting through hands-on projects, fieldwork, or community-based activities.

4. Highlight the value of irreplaceable skills such as creativity, emotional intelligence, and problem-solving, which cannot be easily automated.

5. Incorporate online simulations and virtual case studies to help learners practice applying knowledge in realistic, technology-driven scenarios.

Planning Questions for Real-World Instruction

When you plan your module or lesson unit, keep the following questions in mind. They can help you think more deeply about how to create a real-world learning experience that connects with students' needs and integrates technology effectively.

Objectives and Standards:

1. What are your **real-world learning objectives**?

2. What **driving questions** will engage students and connect to real-world issues?

3. How and when will students discuss **standards**?

4. How will the lessons meet **WIOA expectations** (Workforce Innovation and Opportunity Act), especially for online learners?

5. What are the **main skills** students will practice and master?

Facilitation/Presentation:

1. What **real-world stories** or **examples** will you share?

2. How will you spark your **learners' interest**?

3. How will you activate **prior knowledge**?

4. How will learners develop or access **new factual knowledge**?

5. What **key terms** or **concepts** should learners know?

6. How will learners **contribute** to the lesson as individuals and in groups?

7. What **authentic materials** will students use?

8. How will you monitor **student engagement** and **participation** in an online or hybrid environment?

9. What strategies will you use to create an inclusive, engaging **virtual classroom** that encourages student interaction?

10. How do you plan to **differentiate instruction** to meet the needs of all learners?

Practice:

1. How will you create opportunities for **peer-to-peer learning** in an online or hybrid setting, using both synchronous and asynchronous formats?

2. What **activities** can simulate real-world situations for learning?

3. How will learners **reinforce their learning** and develop their skills over time?

4. What **independent practice** opportunities will students have?

5. What **teamwork practice** opportunities will students have in person and online?

6. How much time will be dedicated to **discussion**, and how will it happen online and in person?

7. How much time will be dedicated to **collaborative projects** in person and virtually?

8. What **speaking** or **presentation** opportunities will students have?

Instructional Technology:

1. How will learners use **technology** for learning, both in-person and online?

2. Which tools or platforms will you use to facilitate **interactive learning**, and how will you ensure all students can access them?

3. How will you manage **technology issues** like internet problems or software glitches during class, and how will you support students in overcoming them?

Evaluation:

1. What **products** will learners create to demonstrate their learning?
2. What **rubrics** will you use for evaluations?
3. What **authentic assessment** will learners have?
4. How will learners demonstrate **critical thinking skills**?
5. How will you measure **deeper learning** and mastery?

Reflection on Learning:

1. How often will learners reflect on the **learning process**?
2. How can you encourage learners to **think deeply** about the material?

CONCLUSION

Leadership is solving problems. The day soldiers stop bringing you their problems is the day you have stopped leading them. They have either lost confidence that you can help or concluded you do not care. Either case is a failure of leadership.

– **Colin Powell**

Now, it's time for you to decide: Do you aspire to be an exceptional team player in adult education? Do you want to make an impact on students' lives? Do you want to make a difference by teaching and fulfilling your commitments to your learners?

It's time to guide learners closer to their dreams—transforming them into the professionals they desire to be. With the instructional ideas you've learned, you can adapt them to get the job done.

This book has encouraged you to take the matter of student retention into your own hands, empowering you to use your true calling in adult ed.

At its core, this book invites you to avoid following the status quo. To quote Seth Godin, "Whatever the status quo is, changing it gives you the opportunity to be remarkable." It's about shifting from compliance-driven instruction to creating engaging, student-centered learning experiences.

All that's left is for you to take concrete actions that will benefit the learners your program seeks to serve. The choices are clear: be average or strive to be remarkable, creating a work of art or compliance work. Make the best decision and prepare your students to conquer real-world challenges ahead, armed with the skills and confidence they need to succeed.

I have a small favor to ask—can you help me spread the word? If you've learned anything from this book, please give a copy to a colleague who has the potential to become remarkable. Don't hesitate to send me questions and comments at teddye@cbledu.com.

Index

Abstract Conceptualization
Active Learning
Active Recall
Andragogy
Andragogical Process Design
Assessment Strategies
Case-based learning (CBL)
Cognitive tasks
Collaborative Learning
Coverage Objectives (COs)
Critical thinking
Deep-structure learning
Differentiated instruction
Distributed Practice
Engagement (Learner engagement)
Student-Centered Learning
Experiential learning
Flexible knowledge
Generalization
Growth mindset
Hybrid learning
Inflexible knowledge
Inquiry-based learning
Learning Objectives (LOs)
Learning systems
Learner experience (LX)
Maslow's hierarchy of needs
Massed practice

Mechanical solutions
Motivation in education
Peer learning
Peer-to-Peer Learning
Prior experience in learning
Problem-based learning (PBL)
Project-based learning (PjBL)
Real-world application, Real-world Learning
Retention (Learner retention)
Rote knowledge
Scaffolding
Self-directed learning
Standardized Testing
Spacing Effect
Storytelling, Story-based Learning
Test-taking Strategies
Theory of Margin
Transformative Learning
Transferable skills
Virtual learning

REFERENCES

Adams, S. (2013). *How to Fail at Almost Everything and Still Win Big: Kind of the Story of My Life.* Penguin.

Adult Education and Literacy. (n.d.). U.S. Department of Education. Retrieved from https://www2.ed.gov/about/offices/list/ovae/pi/AdultEd/index.html?exp=6

Adult learner persistent. (n.d.). *Evidence-based Strategies – Examples, Research and Tools.* Retrieved from https://nelrc.org/persist/counseling_evid_c.html

Clardy, A. (2005). Andragogy: Adult learning and education at its best? *ERIC Online Submission.* Retrieved from https://eric.ed.gov/?id=ED492132

College Board. (2023). *Education pays 2023.* College Board. Retrieved from https://research.collegeboard.org

Collins, J. (2016). *Good to Great: Why Some Companies Make the Leap and Others Don't.* Instaread.

Delisio, E. M. (2002, June 4). What education today means for you tomorrow. *Education World.* Retrieved from https:/www.educationworld.com/a_issues/issue25.htm

DeNeen, J. (2012, October 15). Holistic Teaching: 20 reasons why educators should consider a student's emotional well-being. *InformED.* Retrieved from http://www.opencolleges.edu.au/informed/other/holistic-teaching-20-reasons-why-educators-should-consider-a-students-emotional-well-being/

Dweck, C. S. (2008). *Mindset: The new psychology of success.* Random House Digital, Inc..

Georgetown University Center on Education and the Workforce. (2011). *The college payoff: Education, occupations, lifetime earnings.* Georgetown University. Retrieved from https://cew.georgetown.edu/cew-reports/the-college-pay-off/

Godin, S. (2008). *Tribes: We need you to lead us.* Penguin. New York

Godin, S. (2009). *Purple Cow, New Edition: Transform Your Business by Being Remarkable.* Penguin.

Godin, S. (2018). *This is marketing: You can't be seen until you learn to see.* New York, Portfolio/Penguin.

Hardiman, M. M. (2012). *The brain-targeted teaching model for 21st-century schools.* Corwin Press.

Harlow, W. C. (2003). Bureau of Justice Statistics special report: Education and correctional populations. Retrieved from https://www.bjs.gov/content/pub/pdf/ecp.pdf

Kaiser, H. (n.d.). What Is Problem Solving? *MindTools*. Retrieved from https://www.mindtools.com/pages/article/newTMC_00.htm

Kerka, S. (1988). Strategies for Retaining Adult Students: The Educationally Disadvantaged. *ERIC Digest No. 76.* Retrieved from https://www.ericdigests.org/pre-929/adult.htm

Kilgore, W. (2016, June 20). UX to LX: The Rise of Learner Experience Design. *EdSurge.* Retrieved from https://www.edsurge.com/news/2016-06-20-ux-to-lx-the-rise-of-learner-experience-design

Knowles, M. S. (1980). *The modern practice of adult education: From pedagogy to andragogy.* Cambridge Book Company.

Lynch, M. (2018, December 9). 6 Ways teachers can foster cultural awareness in the classroom. *Huffington Post.* Retrieved from https://www.huffingtonpost.com/matthew-lynch-edd/6-ways-teachers-can-foste_b_6294328.html

McClusky, H. Y. (1963). The course of the adult life span. In W. C. Hallenbeck (Ed.), *Psychology of adults: A handbook for adult education* (pp. 20-28). Adult Education Association of the USA.

McLeod, S. (2005). Maslow's hierarchy of needs. *Simply Psychology*. Retrieved from https://www.simplypsychology.org/maslow.html

McLendon, L., Jones, D., & Rosin, M. (2011). *The return on investment from adult education and training*. McGraw Hill Research Foundation.

Mezirow, J. (1997). Transformative learning: Theory to practice. *New Directions for Adult and Continuing Education*, 1997(74), 5-12.

Nietzel, M. T. (2020, September 9). Low literacy levels among U.S. adults could be costing the economy $2.2 trillion a year. Forbes. Retrieved from https://www.forbes.com/sites/michaelnietzel/2020/09/09/low-literacy-levels-among-us-adults-could-be-costing-the-economy-22-trillion-a-year/

Palmer, P. J. (2017). *The courage to teach: Exploring the inner landscape of a teacher's life* (20th anniversary ed.). Jossey-Bass.

ProLiteracy. (2023). *Adult basic education fact sheet*. Retrieved from https://www.proliteracy.org/wp-content/uploads/2023/09/2023-PL-AdultBasicEducation-FactSheet-2467.pdf

Rachal, J. R. (2002). Andragogy's detectives: A critique of the present and a proposal for the future. *Adult Education Quarterly*, 52(3), 210-227. Retrieved from https://doi.org/10.1177/0741713602052003004

Willingham, D. T. (2002). Ask the Cognitive Scientist Inflexible Knowledge: The First Step to Expertise. *American educator*, 26(4), 31-33.

Willingham, D. T. (2004). "Ask the Cognitive Scientist Practice Makes Perfect, But Only If You Practice Beyond the Point of Perfection." *American Educator* 28, no. 1: 31-33. Retrieved from https://www.aft.org/periodical/american-educator/spring-2004/ask-cognitive-scientist

Willingham, D. T. (2004, Spring). Automaticity in education. *American Federation of Teachers.* https://www.aft.org/ae/spring2004/willingham#:~:text=automaticity%20is%20vital%20in%20education,%2C%20include%20relevant%20detail%2C%20etc.

Willingham, D. T. (2008). What will improve a student's memory? *American Educator*, 32(4), 17-25. Retrieved from https://www.aft.org/sites/default/files/periodicals/wilAutmalingham_0.pdf

Willingham, D. T. (2009). *Why don't students like school?: A cognitive scientist answers questions about how the mind works and what it means for the classroom.* John Wiley & Sons.

World Economic Forum. (2015). *New vision for education: Unlocking the potential of technology.* Retrieved from https://widgets.weforum.org/nve-2015/chapter1.html

MORE TEXTBOOKS BY CBL

ABOUT THE AUTHOR

Teddy Edouard is a Systems and Learning Coach at CBL. He specializes in designing evidence-based training and instructional systems to help adult education programs and instructors increase student engagement, retention, and learning. With over 24 years of experience, he has trained educators and given presentations in more than 30 states.

Coach Teddy holds a Master of Arts in Teaching from the SIT Graduate Institute and a Master of Science in Education (MSEd) in Learning Design and Technology from Purdue University. His expertise spans adult learning, test preparation, instructional design and technology, and systems theory. His research interests include instructional technologies, academic development, adult learning, leadership development, knowledge transfer, and change management.

As a coach and public speaker, he is dedicated to helping professionals and educators adapt to a changing world by building sustainable learning systems and leveraging emerging technologies to foster personal and professional growth.

For more information, visit cbledu.com or contact him at teddye@cbledu.com.

www.ingramcontent.com/pod-product-compliance
Lightning Source LLC
LaVergne TN
LVHW012029060526
838201LV00061B/4527